WAR EAGLE FOREVER!

[signature]

For my little tigers,
Max and Caroline.

www.mascotbooks.com

Touchdown Auburn!

©2022 Kellyn McMahon. All Rights Reserved. No part of this publication may be reproduced, stored in a retrieval system or transmitted in any form by any means electronic, mechanical, or photocopying, recording or otherwise without the permission of the author.

All Auburn University indicia are protected trademarks or registered trademarks of Auburn University and are used under license.

For more information, please contact:
Mascot Books
620 Herndon Parkway, Suite 320
Herndon, VA 20170
info@mascotbooks.com

CPSIA Code: PRT1221A
ISBN-13: 978-1-64543-927-1

Printed in the United States

IT'S FINALLY HERE! Today is the day!
It's my first time seeing the Tigers play!

Football season has begun.
My family is ready for a day of fun!

We dress in colors—
ORANGE and BLUE.
Let's pack the snacks
and grab shakers, too!

We drive to Auburn and
head downtown.
Football fans are all around!

We buy lemonade, so tart and sweet,
then browse the shops on College Street.

Our tailgating tent is by Samford Hall. Let's start the grill and throw the ball.

There are tables full of food. So yummy! I grab a plate and fill my tummy.

At Tiger Walk before the game,
we see the players and shout their names.

I shake my shaker, chant, and cheer!
We give high fives. The game is near!

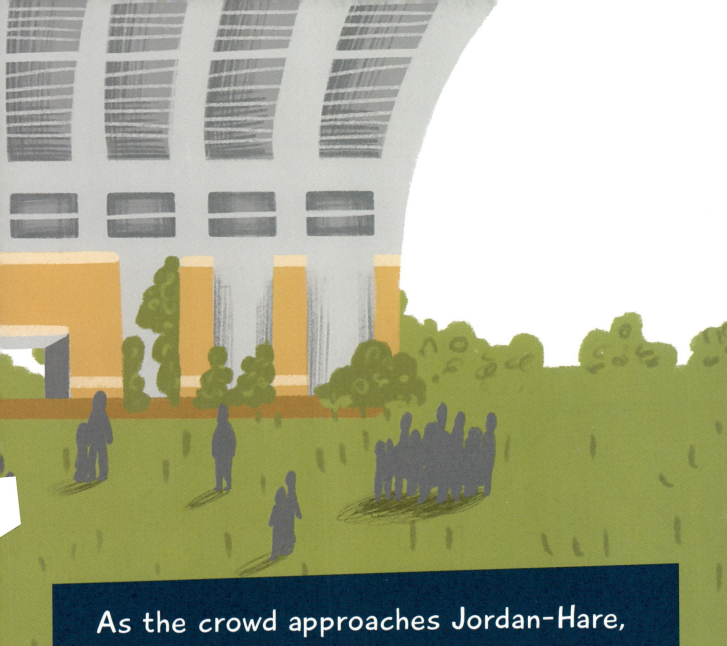

As the crowd approaches Jordan-Hare, excitement is buzzing in the air!

We enter the gates. Wow, what a scene!
Pat-Dye Field is perfectly green!

The lights are on. The crowd is roaring.
My eyes are bright! My heart is soaring!

Before the game, out comes the band.
They march and play—best in the land.

The eagle flies. It's time to play.
"WARRRRRRR EAGLE! HEY!"

Auburn leads in quarter one
after a Tiger touchdown run!

"Bodda getta, bodda getta, bodda getta bah!"
The cheerleaders lead the crowd's hurrah.

Halftime arrives, and the game is tied.
The teams and coaches jog inside.

As Aubie the Tiger makes us laugh,
we get prepared for the second half.

Quarter three goes by so fast,
and quarter four is here at last!

With one play left, the game is still tied.
My belly is full of butterflies!

The ball is hiked. We hold our breath.
The quarterback throws to the left.

The pass is caught! Is this a dream?
"TOUCHDOWN AUBURN!"
We all scream!

We beat the team in red and white. What a game! A special night!

The fans all rush to Toomer's trees to celebrate our victory!

WAR EAGLE, FLY DOWN THE FIELD,
EVER TO CONQUER, NEVER TO YIELD.
WAR EAGLE, FEARLESS AND TRUE.
FIGHT ON YOU ORANGE AND BLUE.
GO! GO! GO!

ON TO VICT'RY, STRIKE UP THE BAND.
HIT 'EM HIGH, HIT 'EM LOW.
STAND UP AND YELL, **HEY!**
WAR EAGLE, WIN FOR **AUBURN**,
POWER OF DIXIELAND!

What a day at **AUBURN U!**
Let's come back next weekend too!

ABOUT THE AUTHOR

Warrrrrrr Eagle! Hey! Kellyn McMahon loves Auburn University and Auburn football. She was born and raised a Tigers fan and wants to share this love with her children and others. She is a 2008 graduate of the Auburn University School of Nursing and lives and works in Birmingham, Alabama. *Touchdown Auburn!* is her first children's book, and she hopes you love this book as much as she does.